BY V.C. THOMPSON

CONSPIRACY THEORIES DEBUNKED

CIVILIZATION WAS RESET

 45TH PARALLEL PRESS

Published in the United States of America by Cherry Lake Publishing

Ann Arbor, Michigan

www.cherrylakepublishing.com

Editorial Consultant: Dr. Virginia Loh-Hagan, EdD, Literacy, San Diego State University

Reading Adviser: Beth Walker Gambro, MS, Ed., Reading Consultant, Yorkville, IL

Photo Credits: © Jessica Rogner, cover, 1, interior graphics; © The Commons/flickr, 4; © Hillbillypirate/Shutterstock, 7; © isoga/Shutterstock, 9; © Dmitry Rukhlenko/Shutterstock, 11; © Lil_Schwarmer/Shutterstock, 13; © NASA, 14; © andras_csontos/Shutterstock, 17; © RHJPhtotos/Shutterstock, 19; © Lestertair/Shutterstock, 21; © Stefano Garau/Shutterstock, 22; © Pecold/Shutterstock, 25; © Artem Avetisyan/Shutterstock, 26

Copyright © 2023 by Cherry Lake Publishing Group

All rights reserved. No part of this book may be reproduced or utilized in any form or by any means without written permission from the publisher.

45th Parallel Press is an imprint of Cherry Lake Publishing Group.

Library of Congress Cataloging-in-Publication Data has been filed and is available at catalog.loc.gov

ABOUT THE AUTHOR

V. C. Thompson is a nurse and author living in Michigan. V. C. is husband to his lovely wife, Anna. Together they are the proud parents of two children, one in Heaven and one newborn. His mission in life is to share his faith through the written word and the healing hand.

TABLE OF CONTENTS

INTRODUCTION 5
CHAPTER 1: THE PREMISE 8
CHAPTER 2: ARTIFACTS DESTROYED 12
CHAPTER 3: NUCLEAR ENERGY AND PLASTICS . . . 16
CHAPTER 4: ATLANTIS STORIES 20
CHAPTER 5: STONEHENGE AND THE PYRAMIDS . . 24
CHAPTER 6: THE VERDICT 29

TRY THIS! 30
LEARN MORE 30
GLOSSARY 31
INDEX 32

Mysteries aren't just for television or books. History is also full of mysteries. One of the biggest mysteries is Roanoke! This happened in the late 1500s. About 115 people disappeared. They left 1 clue. "Croatoan" was carved into a post.

INTRODUCTION

The world is filled with mysteries. Mysteries are things or events that cannot be easily explained. Some mysteries are conspiracies. Conspiracies are secret plans made by a group of people. Most conspiracies are stories that have no evidence. Evidence is proof. It is facts or information that supports a claim. Some conspiracies are later found out to be true. But most conspiracies are false. Sometimes it is hard to tell which conspiracies are true and which are false.

People who believe in conspiracies are called conspiracy theorists. Theorists are people who explain things with ideas called theories. Most people think conspiracy theorists are wrong. Some conspiracy theories are easy to prove wrong. Others are harder to prove wrong. Some are funny. Others are very serious.

Some people call conspiracy theorists crazy or stupid. This is hurtful. It is wrong to attack people, even if what they think is incorrect. Instead, the conspiracy theory should be examined. To examine a conspiracy theory, look at the evidence. Almost every claim has evidence. What matters is *how much* evidence there is and how strong it is. This tells us if the theory is true or false.

Let's take a look at a popular conspiracy theory. Don't forget to keep track of all the evidence. At the end, see if you can debunk this conspiracy yourself!

Most conspiracies have evidence. But the evidence isn't enough.

CHAPTER 1:
THE PREMISE

Modern humans have existed for thousands of years. First, we lived in small groups that moved from place to place. Then we started making camps. These camps grew into tribes. The tribes grew into societies. Eventually, nations, states, and towns grew into civilizations. A civilization is an advanced group of people. Historians name 4 main ancient civilizations. They are ancient Mesopotamia, Egypt, Indus, and China. But what if there were advanced civilizations before these civilizations? What if they were much more advanced?

Doctor Who is the main character of a science-fiction television show. The show is called *Doctor Who*. In the show, Doctor Who is a "Time Lord." He often travels through time. In an episode, he meets an ancient civilization. The people are called Silurians (si-LOOR-ee-uhnz). They had great technology and science. For example, they brought dinosaurs back from extinction. Extinction means dying out. They could also create force fields! Force fields are walls that are invisible.

Is this just a fantasy or myth? Maybe not. What if there was a society like the Silurians? Is there a way to know if a 100-million-year-old civilization existed? This is called the Silurian hypothesis. A hypothesis is an educated guess. This hypothesis states we're not the first advanced civilization. The hypothesis is named after the show.

The mud flood theory is another conspiracy. It says there was an ancient empire called Tartaria. Tartaria was advanced. They built many things. They built the pyramids of Egypt. They built the Great Wall of China. But a mud flood destroyed the Tartarian people.

SPOT-

PLATO

Plato is a famous philosopher. A philosopher is someone who studies life's big questions. Plato lived from 428 to 348 BCE in Athens, Greece. Plato was perhaps the first to talk about advanced ancient civilizations. He even wrote a book about it. He talked about an advanced society called Atlantis. Plato's student, Aristotle, thought that the story was fake. But another philosopher, Crantor, thought it was real. Philosophy experts believe Plato invented Atlantis to prove a point. They say he used it to describe the dangers of political power.

LIGHT

The Silurian hypothesis is similar to the story of Atlantis. The story of Atlantis is very old. It dates back more than 2,000 years. This conspiracy states that civilization was reset. It says human-like people lived long before humans. They were more advanced than we are. But they disappeared. Some believe they all died in a catastrophic event. A catastrophe is a disaster that causes a lot of destruction. Like the dinosaurs, these people all died. It was so long ago that their cities were buried. Almost all the evidence is gone. Or is it? There is a great deal of evidence for this conspiracy. Let's examine it further.

CHAPTER 2:
ARTIFACTS DESTROYED

THE CONSPIRACY

There are no artifacts of an advanced ancient civilization. Artifacts are old objects. Is a lack of evidence proof that a civilization never existed?

What happens when you don't clean your room? After a few weeks, dust covers everything. The same happens with Earth. As years pass, Earth's surface is covered with new soil. The new soil crushes the old soil. Eventually, the old soil forms a hard layer. These layers are called strata. Strata are the layers that form Earth's surface.

Archaeologists are scientists who study past civilizations. They study ancient artifacts and human remains. They also

Old artifacts are often found deep in the ground. These ancient vessels were discovered in Greece.

The oldest artifact was found in Kenya. The stone tool is over 3.3 million years old. Pictured is the area where it was found.

study human and animal fossils. Fossils are bones or imprints that become rock. Archaeologists do this by digging hundreds and hundreds of feet down. They know when the human fossils lived by what layer of Earth they're in. Archaeologists know how advanced past societies were. They look at the tools the civilizations left behind.

However, Silurians lived so long ago that any artifacts they left behind would be too deep in Earth. The weight of the other layers would be too heavy. All Silurian artifacts would be turned to dust!

DEBUNKED

It is unlikely that any unknown advanced civilization existed before us. But let's say it did. Their artifacts would be crushed by now. Any trace of them would be very hard to find. It would be even harder if a meteoroid killed them. A meteoroid is a rock from space that enters Earth. Not having evidence is not evidence that they existed. However, it's unlikely they existed without us knowing.

CHAPTER 3:
NUCLEAR ENERGY AND PLASTICS

THE CONSPIRACY

Advanced civilizations use advanced things. This includes plastic and nuclear energy. People have found evidence of these advanced things. Researchers found plastic in hidden places where there weren't humans. They also found plastic at ancient sites. Plastic is hard to destroy. Plastic is made using special technology. It lasts for a long time. It doesn't decompose quickly. Decompose means to break down.

Nuclear energy is made by splitting atoms. Atoms are the smallest parts of an element. Splitting atoms is hard. Scientists discovered how to do it in the 1930s. But researchers believe Africa had access to nuclear power 2 billion years ago! Scientists found evidence of ancient nuclear waste. Nuclear waste is the leftover of nuclear energy. It is no longer useful. But it can be dangerous.

We found evidence of ancient plastic and nuclear energy. Is this proof that an advanced civilization like the Silurians existed?

Ancient plastic was made using the same ingredients as asphalt! Our roads are made of asphalt. The Chumash tribe made ancient plastic. They did this as early as 5,000 years ago!

SPOT-LIGHT

BRAIN BLIND SPOTS

Cars have blind spots. Our eyes have blind spots. Our brains have blind spots too! This is called the Dunning-Kruger effect. It is named after 2 psychologists, David Dunning and Justin Kruger. Psychologists are doctors who study human emotions and behavior.

The effect is when people overestimate their understanding of something. People with less knowledge of a subject think they know more than they do. They aren't aware of their lack of knowledge. Experts underestimate their knowledge. They know there is always more to learn.

An example of this would be talent shows like *American Idol*. Some people who try out have great voices. Then there are people who just can't sing. But they think they can! This is true for conspiracy theories. People who believe conspiracies think they know the answers. They think they have evidence. But they might just be falling for the Dunning-Kruger effect. They don't know what they don't know.

DEBUNKED

Plastic is proof of modern technology. Modern technology is proof of an advanced civilization. But the plastic found in hidden places was produced by modern humans. There was plastic found in Midway Atoll near Hawaii. Only animals live in this area. Humans don't live there. So why is there plastic? Unfortunately, the area attracts the plastic from other places. This isn't evidence of the Silurians. But it is evidence we need to help clean up Earth.

The nuclear waste in Africa is not human-made. It's caused by nature! The area is called the Oklo-Formation. It has a large amount of uranium. Uranium is an element used to create nuclear energy. It is found in nuclear waste. But it is also found naturally in water, soil, and rock.

19

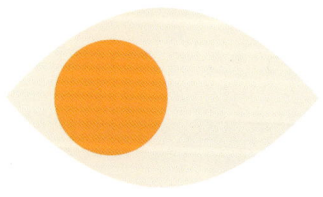

CHAPTER 4:
ATLANTIS STORIES

THE CONSPIRACY

Many stories are told about the lost civilization of Atlantis. Greek philosopher Plato was the first person to talk about Atlantis. Many people connect Atlantis to aliens. They believe Atlantis was a society of aliens. Today, there is talk about aliens on Mars. Mars is the fourth planet in our solar system.

Could the stories of Atlantis be about aliens? Did they move to Mars?

The story of Atlantis is told in *Timaeus* and *Critias*. Plato wrote these around 360 BCE.

Many believe the people of Atlantis weren't even human! Some believe they were half god and half human. Others believe they were aliens.

22

DEBUNKED

Stories of advanced ancient civilizations are common. But these are just stories made up by people. For example, Plato made up his story of Atlantis to teach his students. He wanted to show what a utopian society is. A utopia is an imaginary place where everything is perfect.

Could there be aliens on Mars, though? Yes and no. The answer to this isn't black and white. There could be aliens, but not in the way we think. Astronomers recently sent cameras to Mars. Astronomers are scientists who study space. The videos of Mars show no signs of intelligent life. But there is evidence of water and other molecules that are linked to life. That indicates that the planet once could have supported some form of life.

23

CHAPTER 5:
STONEHENGE AND THE PYRAMIDS

THE CONSPIRACY

The world has many structures that look impossible to build. One of these is Stonehenge. Stonehenge is a prehistoric monument in England. It is a circle of huge stones. Each stone is about 13 feet (4 meters) tall and 7 feet (2.1 m) wide. They each weigh about 25 tons. That's the weight of more than 12 cars!

The stones were carved into the same shape. Then they were planted upright in the ground. Stonehenge is more than 5,000 years old. People 5,000 years ago didn't have the equipment we have. So how was Stonehenge built?

The largest Stonehenge stone weighs about 30 tons. That's about the weight of 15 elephants!

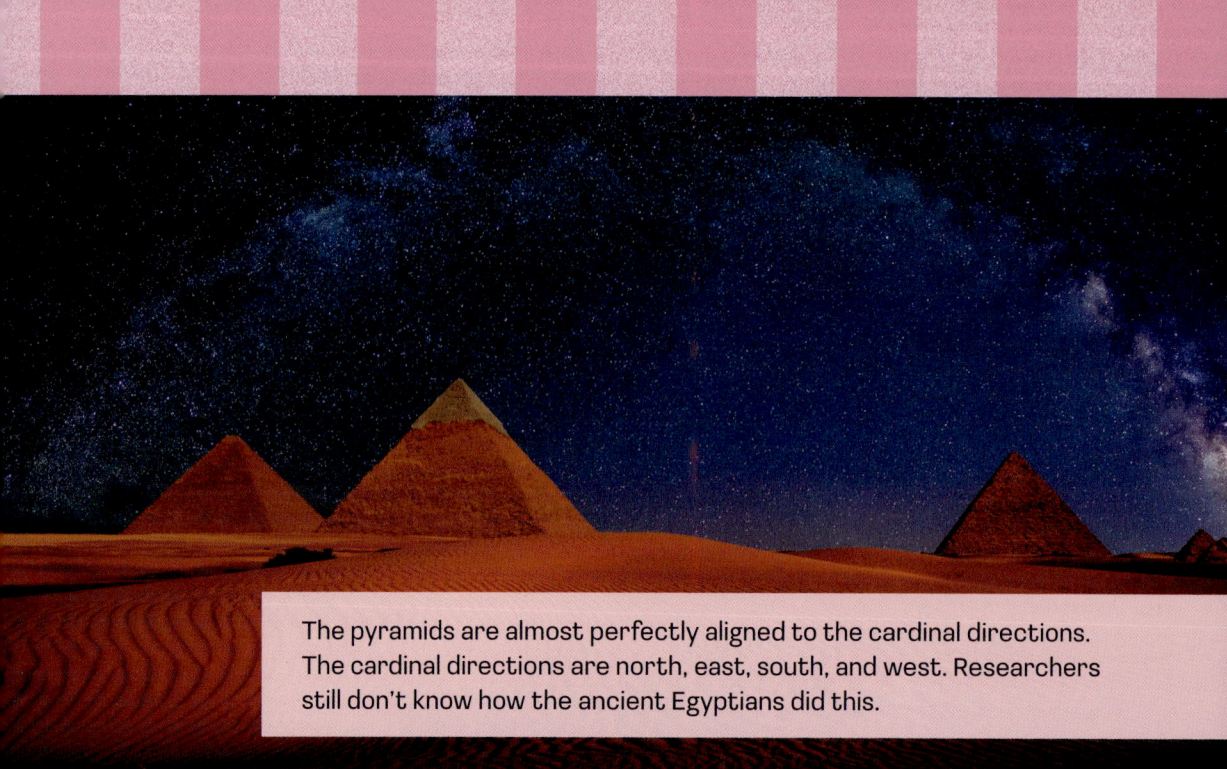

The pyramids are almost perfectly aligned to the cardinal directions. The cardinal directions are north, east, south, and west. Researchers still don't know how the ancient Egyptians did this.

The story of the pyramids of Egypt is similar. The Great Pyramid of Giza is 481 feet (147 m) tall. It is built of more than 2 million huge stones! Together, the stones weigh 6 million tons! Each was carved to the same shape and size. Then they were stacked on each other. Inside are tunnels and rooms. The pyramid is 4,500 years old. How is this possible? There were no construction machines back then . . . or were there?

Were the Silurians responsible for building Stonehenge and the pyramids?

DEBUNKED

Stonehenge and the pyramids are truly remarkable. In fact, they are ancient wonders of the world! But that doesn't mean that they were built by an advanced ancient civilization.

The ancient Egyptians built the pyramids. There are a few theories of how they did this. The most common theory is that they used sleds. They placed sleds under the stones to drag them. They then used ramps to slide them up the pyramid. The large stones were pushed and pulled up the ramps. Thousands of Egyptian workers helped make this possible.

Stonehenge is similar. People probably used sleds to roll the stones to the area. Then they may have dug holes to stand the holes upright. They could have used ropes to hoist the stones into the holes. Hoist means to raise or lift something. Then they probably used ramps to stack the top stones. Building Stonehenge likely took a very long time. Experts believe there were 5 phases of construction. They think it took at least 1,500 years to build Stonehenge.

SPOT-

HYPOTHESIS

Hypothesizing is an important tool used in critical thinking. Hypothesizing is when you propose a possible explanation. Critical thinking involves always asking questions. It involves looking at evidence. Before you hypothesize, you have to have a question. For example, Adele wants to know why fireflies light up. She hypothesizes fireflies do it to talk to each other. Adele is at least partially right. Some fireflies do light up to find mates. Others light up to warn predators.

In this conspiracy, the question is if pre-human societies existed. The Silurian hypothesis is one explanation. Another explanation is that they existed but were not advanced. Another theory is that no societies existed before ours. Can you think of other hypotheses?

LIGHT

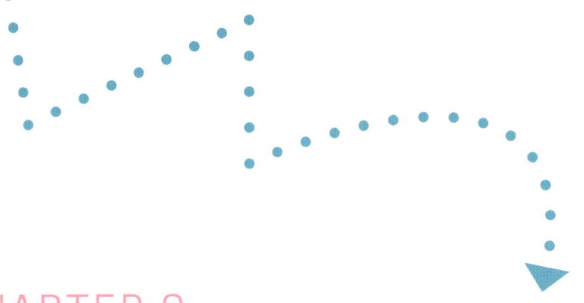

CHAPTER 6:
THE VERDICT

Civilization being reset is an exciting conspiracy. It is fun to imagine a pre-human civilization. There are so many interesting questions. Why are there no Silurian artifacts? Where did the plastic and nuclear waste come from? How do you explain all the stories of past civilizations? And who built Stonehenge and the pyramids?

There are, of course, easy answers to these questions. There are no Silurian artifacts because they never existed. Plastic came from modern humans. Ancient nuclear waste naturally occurs. The stories of past civilizations were just stories. And creative ancient humans built Stonehenge and the pyramids over a very long period of time.

The Silurians are fun to think about. But they aren't real. They only exist in television shows like *Doctor Who*. The evidence supports this conclusion. This conspiracy theory has been DEBUNKED. Or has it? What do you think?

TRY THIS!

1. With a parent's permission, dig a small hole in your backyard. Look for artifacts! Don't have a backyard? Research public spaces where you can dig.

2. Write your own science-fiction story. Like Plato, tell a story of a past civilization. What technology did they have? How did they die out?

3. Watch the Silurian episode of *Doctor Who* with your parents. Is such a civilization possible?

LEARN MORE

Corso, Phil. *Conspiracy Theories and Fake News.* New York, NY: PowerKids Press, 2018.

Goldstein, Margaret J. *What Are Conspiracy Theories?* Minneapolis, MN: Lerner Publications, 2020.

Johnson, Anna Maria. *Debunking Conspiracy Theories.* New York, NY: Cavendish Square Publishing, LLC, 2019.

Loh-Hagan, Virginia. *Creepy Conspiracy Theories.* Ann Arbor, MI: Cherry Lake Publishing, 2018.

GLOSSARY

archaeologists (ar-kee-AH-luh-jists) scientists who study past civilizations

artifacts (AR-tih-fakts) old objects made by humans

astronomers (uh-STRAH-nuh-muhrs) scientists who study space

atoms (AA-tuhmz) the smallest parts

catastrophic (kah-tuh-STRAH-fik) describing a major disaster

civilizations (sih-vuh-luh-ZAY-shuhnz) advanced societies

conspiracies (kuhn-SPIHR-uh-seez) secret plans to do something bad or against the law

decompose (dee-kuhm-POHZ) break down

evidence (EH-vuh-duhnss) facts or information that support a claim

extinction (ik-STING-shuhn) process of dying out

fossils (FAH-suhl) a trace or print or the remains of a plant or animal of a past age preserved in Earth or rock

hypothesis (hye-PAH-thuh-suhs) guess or possible explanation

meteoroid (MEE-tee-uh-royd) a rock from space that enters Earth's atmosphere

mysteries (MIH-stuh-reez) things that are unknown or hard to explain

philosopher (fuh-LAH-suh-fuhr) person who studies questions and ideas about knowledge and right and wrong

psychologists (sye-KAH-luh-jists) doctors who study human emotions and behavior

strata (STRAH-tuh) layers that form Earth's surface

theorists (THEE-uh-rists) people who explain things with ideas called theories

uranium (yoo-RAY-nee-uhm) element used to create nuclear energy

utopian (yoo-TOH-pee-uhn) something that is unrealistically perfect

INDEX

aliens, 20, 23
ancient civilizations, 8, 10, 12, 15, 24, 26, 29
ancient wonders of the world, 24–27
archaeology, 12–15
Aristotle, 10
artifacts, 12–13, 14, 15
asphalt, 17
astronomers, 23
Atlantis, 10, 20–23

catastrophic events, 11, 15
civilization reset theory
    backstory, 8–9
    beliefs and theories, 11, 12, 15, 16, 20, 24–26, 28, 29
conspiracies, 5, 6
conspiracy theorists, 6, 18
Crantor, 10
critical thinking, 28

debunking and disproving, 29
    artifacts theory, 15
    Atlantis theory, 23
    plastic and nuclear energy theory, 19
    Stonehenge and pyramids theory, 27

disappearances, 4
disaster events, 11, 15
Doctor Who, 8, 29
Dunning, David, 18
Dunning-Kruger effect, 18

Egyptian pyramids, 26, 27
energy sources, 16, 19
evidence, 5, 6, 7, 16, 18, 28

fossils, 15

history writing and erasing, 9
human civilizations
    history, 8, 12–15
    hypotheses, 8–9, 11, 12, 15, 16, 29
    study, 12–15
hypothesizing, 28

knowledge, 18
Kruger, Justin, 18

Mars, 20, 23
meteoroids, 15
mud flood theory, 9
mysteries, 4, 5

nuclear energy and waste, 16, 19

personal attacks, 6
philosophers, 10
plastics, 16–17, 19
Plato, 10, 20, 21, 23
pyramids, 26–27

Roanoke Colony, 4

self-awareness, 18
Silurian hypotheses, 8–9, 10, 11, 12, 16, 26, 28, 29
Stonehenge, 24–27
stone tools, 14

technology, 16–17, 19, 26, 27

uranium, 19
utopias, 23